Other books by K.L. Bye

Deadly Presents

Forget them not!
Blessings
Kael

a step from heaven

For information contact:
Turtle Run Publishing
P.O. Box 267
Circle Pines, MN 55014

trp77519@skypoint.com
http://www.skypoint.com/~trp77519

Logo art: Bekah Bye
Cover and Illustrations: Frank Schaffer
Back cover map: Frank Schaffer. Used by permission.
Foreword: Nelson DeMille

ISBN: 0-9641975-0-3

Library of Congress Card Catalog Number: 96-90146

Printed in the United States of America

Praises for A Step From Heaven

"*A Step From Heaven* is very much as a day in Vietnam, seemingly peaceful and quiet only to be shattered by the realities of the horrors of war."

Frank Schaffer
1st Aviation Brigade, US Army

"*A Step From Heaven* is **exactly** the way we all felt."

LZ Bluegrass, KY

"A unique book of poetry about a time in America's history presented in an interesting and unique manner. I recommend this book to anyone who wants to know the true meaning of Vietnam."

Richard Johnson
Lt. Col. USA (Ret.)

"I was just stunned when I started reading *A Step From Heaven*. Who is this woman to get it so right? Where did she get the knowledge that so many of us have, but could never express? With unerring accuracy she understands and writes the feelings of America's warriors."

Chris Noel
Author/Actress/AFRV '66-71

"*A Step From Heaven* brought back some memories. Some good. Some not so good. Nevertheless, as a person who could not get into reading poetry before, I read every page and felt the words."

Jerry Bailin
J2, MACV
Tan Son Nhut Air Base

Introduction

"K L Bye has created an unusual, but not all unpleasant relationship between the flashbacks that Vietnam Veterans sometimes experience and this--her second--book of poetry about soldiers of the 60's and 70's, their war and Vietnam. The relationship is created through minimalist use of words which carry an import far beyond their superficial meanings.

Take the phrase 'FNG' for instance. Three letters that conjure flashbacks of getting off an airplane and walking into the unknown and--365 days later--getting out of the horrible reality of the war and onto another, homeward bound, plane.

Bye's poetry is evocative. The words of her poetry are sparse, spare, lean and taut, but the memories the words recreate are anything but that.

The images and sensations of Vietnam flood back, if you've been there. To others, the words are equally evocative--playbacks of newsreels, television programs, movies, books, conversations with veterans.

Regardless of which experience the reader best relates to, it's interesting to note that there is a definite absence of rancor in Bye's writing. These poems don't blame, particularly; nor do they condemn. They are-at one level-merely words. But one would be well advised to look beyond the mere words, however, and let the wash of emotion, memory, recollection and pain expand to fill the available consciousness.

Illustrations which are reminiscent of Bill Maudlin's *Willie and Joe* only complement the words.

If you were there, this will be a memory jogger; if you were not, it will help you understand what it was really like."

Mike Scott, USA '68-69

Foreward

In her Vietnam poetry, K L Bye, who is a woman and who was not there, speaks directly to me, a man who *was* there.

Bye shows a remarkable understanding of the war, the psyches of those who served, the very heart of darkness of this ill-fated adventure.

Just as Stephen Crane was able to write *Red Badge of Courage* without having served in the Civil War, so K L Bye is able to step back, understand Vietnam with a writer's eye and a poet's soul, then create with deep passion and emotion, perhaps better than a veteran could.

These are truly remarkable poems, heartfelt, savvy, simpatico, and above all, right on. There's hardly a middle-aged man or woman in America who won't nod in recognition when reading Bye's evocative words: the sixties and seventies come alive for a brief few minutes as we read, then recede again into that poignant place in our minds; but now the memories are better illuminated, and can be better expressed if we should need to express any of that time to our children.

A truly powerful collection of poetry and feelings, memories that will make you sad and some that will make you smile.

Nelson DeMille

NOTEWORTHY THANKS

Thank you--
    Nelson DeMille for reminding me "This is
the season for writing". I will keep a screen on it.

Thank you--
    Frank Schaffer for your perceptive artwork
and for your input. I couldn't have done it without you.

Thank you--
    Mike Scott for the lasting impression of
Nam through pictures and narratives that en-
deared me to Nam so many years ago.

Thank you--
    "Big Al" for your encouraging words, at just
the right time, and for being the Bro' I never had.

Thank you--
    To the Giver of Life for allowing me to
share the pain of the Nam Brothers.

K L Bye
March 21, 1996

With love for

"Mad Mike"
"Big Al"
and
"Sarge"

In memory of
"Long" John Silver
and
James "Tony" Koch

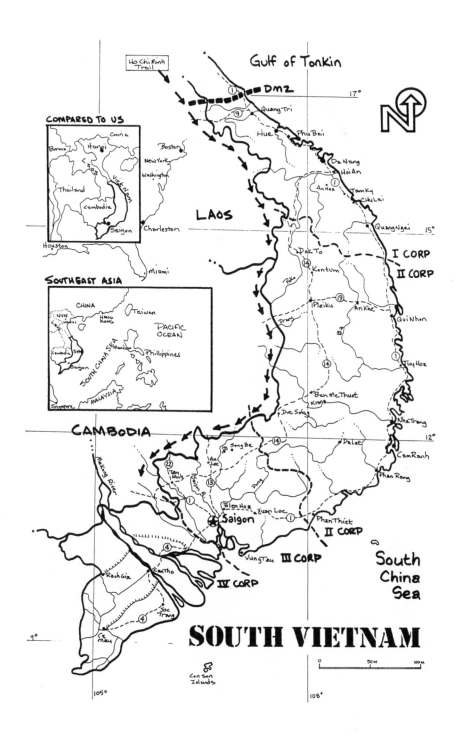

Ho Chi Minh Trail

Gulf of Tonkin

DMZ

17°

COMPARED TO US

China
Burma   Hanoi   Boston
                  New York
Thailand Viet Nam Washington
     Cambodia
          Saigon Charleston
Houston
              Miami

LAOS

Quang Tri
Hue   Phu Bai

Da Nang
Hoi An
An Hoa   Tam Ky
                Chu Lai

Quang Ngai   15°

SOUTHEAST ASIA

CHINA   Taiwan
NVN   Hanoi Hong Kong
              PACIFIC
Cambodia SVN   OCEAN
     Saigon   SOUTH CHINA SEA Manila
                    Phillipines
          Singapore MALAYSIA

Dak To
Kontum   I CORP
                II CORP

Pleiku   An Khe
Drang   Qui Nhon

Tuy Hoa

Ban Me Thuot
Krong

Duc Song   Nha Trang

CAMBODIA

Song Be
     An   Da Lat   12°
     Loc
Tay 13
Ninh   CamRanh
                Phan Rang
Bien Hoa
     Xuan Loc
  Saigon
          Phan Thiet   II CORP

Vung Tau III CORP   South
                      China
Rach Gia CanTho   Sea
          IV CORP
     Soc Trang

Ca Mau

9°

Con Son
Islands

SOUTH VIETNAM

0   50M   100M

105°   108°

" ...the beginning of the end of war is in remembrance..."

Herman Wouk
The Winds of War

never told

basic training
boot camp
home leave
all day raining

time too short
tears shed
hugs all around
gotta report

on bird to fly
10,000 miles
to be fng
hope to God
i don't die

bill of goods sold
no way to win
politicians waging proud
real story never told

never told

" We are not going to send American boys nine or ten thousand miles away from home to do what Asian boys ought to be doing for themselves."

President Lyndon Baines Johnson
October 12, 1964

welcome to vietnam

c-rats
and
kia stats

m-sixteens
and
jungle greens

didi mow
and
taken pow

the citadel
and
hot hell

china beach
and
out of reach

fire fight
and
vc night

tan son nhut
and
kicked butt

toe tags
and
body bags

welcome to vietnam

o j t

yup

take a young kid
shave his head
stick 'im in basic

teach 'im how
to play soldier
then stick 'im
on a plane
drop 'im off in nam

on the job training
begins yesterday
green recruits
press noses against
the window pane
of seasoned warriors
wanting to be
one of the guys

the right is earned

off to war we go

heigh-ho heigh-ho
it's off to war we go

doc tries to gather blood spilled
to put it back where it belongs
curses don't make good bandages

bashful's react time
blew him to kingdom come
nothin' left
just a memorial service

grumpy went on a rampage
blood soaked dear john
clutched tightly
in a detached fist

dopey always screwin' around
claimin' this is all a dream
ak-47 chewed 'im to pieces
now he's somebody's dream

sleepy let guard down
throat slit from ear to ear
sleepin' with warriors fallen

sneezy and recon don't mix
aahhchoo echoes pinpoint location
fire fight hell breaks loose
bullet to the throat
silences forever aahhchoo

happy always smilin'
day and a wake up
mortar round woke
him up in heaven

heigh-ho heigh-ho
off to war we go
seven dwarfs
are no more

journey to this valley

a journey to this valley i take
beware of deadly punji stake

a journey to this valley i march
thankful mama-san uses no starch

a journey to this valley i cross
all too certain there will be loss

a journey to this valley i crawl
as a soldier to give my all

a journey to this valley i fight
hacking jungle away to light

a journey to this valley i cry
give me ten good reasons why

a journey to this valley i fear
strong sense ambush is near

a journey to this valley i trod
forever scared-is there a God

a journey to this valley i make
help us God this earth to shake

a journey to this valley to die
comfort those sure to cry

a journey to this valley of strife
i found again my life

flying spoon

cautious sloshing
across the stream
i wanna scream

no moon
no street lights
cat eyes i could use

calculated steps
up the river bank
into tall grass

watchful eye
for trip wire glimmer
flying spoon

too late

yakety-yak

yakety yak

damn

thought it was a hit song
just ak–47 talkin' back

flashes from the tree line
look like giant fire flies
flickering to be caught

no catching them and
putting them in a jar
with holes in the lid

no sir

only holes are gonna be in us
don't get a jar with a lid
bag with a zipper and a toe tag

yakety yak

i talk back

nightmare

rising mist
early mornin'
wake up call

what will
the day
hold for us

      stand down
      beer sippin'
      card playin'
      boredom
      itchin'
      for action
      laughter

ambush
heavy casualties
air strikes
fierce dying cries
bits and pieces

another nightmare in vietnam

tunnel rat

pistol and a flashlight
arms a tunnel rat

hole in the ground
invites a look
fire in the hole

traffic rules

sliver of moonlight
sneakin' down'
the middle of the river
like a white line
on a two lane highway

where's the no passing zone
aren't we s'posed to obey
the traffic rules

hell what am i sayin'
there are no rules here
no passing double yellow line
no yield to pedestrian
in the crosswalk

we jay walk
across the stream
guns ready to blaze away
and blast anything that moves
that isn't us

monsoon malady

rain poncho
floppy hat
waterlogged boots

leaky
waterproof gear
monsoon season in nam

breath away

triple layer canopy jungle
nothin' can penetrate this mass
takes on a life of its own

what lurks in the shadows
charlie, frankenstein's dog
boogie men, politicians

fine tread sandaled feet
black pajama clad bodies
fingertip toting death

a breath away
from heaven

reassurance

honest
mom
it's
not
that
bad
here
don't
worry
i'll
be
okay

boom

memories

past memories

mustangs and t-birds
girls in tight sweaters
and poodle skirts
football practice late august
bullwinkle and rocky
gunsmoke and bonanza
baseball trading cards
my trombone
and marching band

future memories

whole villages torched
screams of terror
whomp–whomp–whomp
mortar whistles
leeches
three layer jungle canopy
boom, boom, boom
buddies blown to hell
cries of the dead

life long ago

turning nineteen

woke
to
a
whistle
and
thud

earth
moving
boom
and
geckos
screaming
naughty
words

is
this
any
way
to
turn
nineteen

different music

do-wah do-wah do-wah
chorus to any song
if you don't know the words

boom-bah boom-bah boom-bah
song and dance of arty
kicking butt on victor charles

spooks

spooks
    scare the crap
        right outa ya

spooks
    bad news guys
        down and dirty

spooks
    suck you in
        hang you out to dry

spooks
    conducting
        shady business
            no credentials

spooks
    covert operations
        successful death

spooks
    well known secret
        how dumb are we

spooks
    mia
        pow's

we knew you not

rising mist

daybreak finds steam rising
in a heavy mist from the jungle
releasing fears of what
the day will bring
death and destruction
good news of going home
lost buddies rescued
what will the day bring

silence will soon be shattered by
booms and whomp-whomps
cries of the fallen
screams of the innocents
rat-a-tat-tats
and unprintable oaths

sweet freshly scrubbed
smiling faces of girls
left behind come
to mind as the day
prepares itself for what will be

God help me make it through
another day of hell

chopper down

smoke
charred
the sky

just
above
the tree tops

etched
for
all to see

death
hung
in the air

chopper

d

o

w

n

shooting gallery

running along
on top of the dike
like ducks in a shooting
gallery at the fair

step right up
take your best shot
knock down three
ducks in a row
win the lovely
lady a prize
c'mon folks don't be shy
five shots for a buck

charlie must have been to
the fair and paid his
five shots for a buck
water and dirt never looked
so good as a refuge it became

good thing charlie was a
poor shot that day

someone's weeping

sloshing down stream
guns at the ready
eyes watchin' from river bank
never takin' advantage given

smell ambush
a peaceful oasis
turned soon to
cracks and chatters

caught in open
cover sought
stream runs red

sudden quiet
someone's weeping
a world away

mosquito bait

standard issue green
spit polished boots
almost new issue weapon
trompin' off to the bush
to impress the enemy

sweat stains green
crisp uniform wilted
muddy high shine boots
flak jackets become
sleeveless shirts

they didn't tell us
we'd be lunch for
mosquitoes and leeches
have our feet rot
go for weeks without
showers and real food

what kind of war is this
they never told us
we wouldn't win—
couldn't win

ak'd down

captain of the football team
damn new guy and green

fifty yards rushing
much blood gushing

king of homecoming dance
surviving nam mostly chance

wore cloak and crown
half my unit ak'd down

danced the night away
sorry nam, don't wanna stay

kissed my janie goodnight
uncle sam insists i fight

came the dawn
i fought, now i'm gone

rivers of tears fall
my name now on the Wall

before another war makes haste
let not our lives be waste

medic

medic! he cried
sucking air
can't see, man
gettin' dark

medic! he cried
ragged breathing
torrent of blood
rapidly ebbing life

medic! he cried
stretching out a stump
one last gasp for air

mom! he cried
closed his eyes
and died

sir

dig in
move out
up and down
round and round
lock and load

yes sir
no sir
right away sir

medic!

damn

sittin' in my tankety-tank
revvin' up my engine
rarin' to drag highway one
shoot charlie's blankety-blank

damn

how to open the latchety-latch
ungodly hot and stuffy
like an oven
bakin' cookies by the batchety-batch

layin' down trackety-track
movin' merrily along
squashin' everything like bugs
a fly swatter goin' whackety-whack

damn

machine gun yakety-yak
cover from above
about time
tired of all this flackety-flack

wish i could be backety-back
base camp
world would be better
where there's no lackety-lack

tankety-tank
trackety-track
don't wanna go
backety-back
jack

intended

broken toys
childhood joys

intended wife
warrior's life

shattered dreams
fallens screams

big spender

religious right, left, right
out of step with the world
stone gods offer no help
prayers for the dead
offer no help

we are no gods
we offer help
to rid a country of a
raging threat

we offer a gift of freedom
no real takers
just big spenders of
lives not their own

dead wrong right

truth
justice
american way

never were told the truth
no justice whatsoever
american way all right

dead wrong right

distant weeping

hot
sleepless
scary
night

charlie's
smell
permeates
air

shadows
slice
through
blackness

death
prowls
strengthened
perimeter

body
parts
scattered
airborne

distant
weeping
loudly
proclaimed

everywhere red

distant voices
drawing closer
sing-song nva

hidden along river bank
ragged nerves
patience practiced

closer, closer
sing-song, sing-song
very unaware

drenching sweat
pounding heart
wait unbearable

open fire
m-16 chatter
open fire

ripped flesh
body parts
everywhere red

heart beat

a heart beat
so strong
so precious
so full of promise

whine of mortar

a heart beat
so rapid
so jumpy
so scared

frags of shrapnel

a heart beat
so weak
so slow
so still

a heart beat—
gone

dawn of remembrance

gotta get some r and r
get me a woman
a bottle of booze
and a night to forget

forget

the blood
raining body pieces
screams for medic
horror of torching
entire village
hearing cries of
women and children dying

forget

terror of the night
the lp
incoming-outgoing
firecracker lit sky

zooming tracers for a mark
hot lz's
dust off

forget

green lt. callin' fire
on his own
best friend blown to bits
callous attitude riding
herd on emotions

yeah

r and r
a woman
good booze
a night to forget
before dawn of remembrance

my girl

red hair brown eyes
sexy body in a mini skirt
fun lovin' my girl
safe in the world
from this hell on earth

will she still want me
when i come home
not the boy she hugged
tightly good-bye
but a middle aged man
embittered by the hell
he's gone through

will she still want me

broken promise

steam bath night
            jungle rot

satin skin marilou
            tender touch

benjo stench heat
            victor charles

soft curves felt
            kisses returned

trip wire hidden
            body parts

silky blond hair
            smellin' good

kingdom come blown
            body bag

tear stained marilou
            broken heart
                  broken promise

simple pleasures

warm embrace
    hot meal
        hot shower
            clean sheets

real bed
    simple things
        complex war

when again hello

ragged snapshot
looked at a thousand times

    lifesaver

promises of marriage
spoken to himself

    sanity preserver

lifetime ago good-bye
when again hello

peace man

make love not war
hippies goin' to san francisco
with flowers in their hair
love beads strung
around their neck
long hair down to wherever

    peace man

love don't stop bullets
or mortars or claymores
or grenades or punji stakes

    peace man

wish we all could go to san fran
 with flowers in our hair
but we've gone into
hell with a flak jacket
and dog tags markin' time
till we're short and on that
silver bird back to the world

gonna get me some love beads
let my hair grow
find my way to san francisco

    make love not war

    wish i could man

"War hath no fury like a non-combatant."

E. C. Montague

for sale

for sale
foreign real estate
needs cleanfiill
best offer
call hanoi
evenings

madness

guns a-blazin'
sky rainin'
dirt and body parts

how many takes
does it take
to end this
madness

where's the director
why isn't he yelling
cut

holy shit
this ain't no movie
damn

numbah one

joe numbah one
by day

joe numbah ten
by night

where is the enemy
all around us

are we our own enemy
no one can find the enemy

charlie's playin'
button, button,
who's got the button

mask

a peaceful people
stuck in a cauldron
of hate and power
stirred by oppression
and some far left or
right faction determined
to have their way

friendly by day
deadly by night
so two faced
who to trust
smiling faces
trusting eyes
mask the lies lived

what's the point
in fighting another minute
blow the hell out
of this country
and let's go
back to the world

hollywood lied

must've been out of my mind
to join this madness

what was i thinking
for god's sake

should be home workin' my tail off
to stay out of this hell hole

jeez why didn't i go to canada
can i get there from here

war ain't what it's cracked up to be
hollywood lied

"It's the inherent right of the government to lie to save itself."

Asst. Sec. of Defense
Arthur D. Sylvester,
Dec. 6, 1962

ain't no textbook war

breath sucking
benjo empowered heat
mandate for sweat
and target practice

we're the targets
they need the practice

glistening shirtless skin
trickles beads of sweat
to the waist band
heat rash

never dried out boots
hurry jungle rot feet
anything dry is suspicious

move out and over
around and through
wind up back
where we started
flunked compass 101

take same ground seven times
give it back eight
movies always win
in one battle

this ain't no textbook war

remnants of sanity

night comes to steal
remnants of sanity

peering into the darkness
can't see to save my soul
black on black on black

sudden movement to the left
gun points in that direction
nerves on edge

sudden movement to the right
my God they're all over the place
gun points in that direction

calm suddenly captures me

sudden movement to the left
just my heart beating hard

night comes to steal
remnants of sanity

red

red
stains green dark
red
tie-dyes white
red
sticky mess
red
soaks the soul
in
remembrance
in
violation
in
defiance

sandals

ho chi minh
sandals
gonna get
g.i. boot
clear
to
china

dangerous

hide 'n' seek
dangerous game

shoot at nothing
kill innocent people

or are they

rearrange landscape
easy get in and out
just a target

whose dumb idea was this

unfinished business

recon
dear john

m-16
returned ring

ammo belt
hurt felt

forever changed

courage left
like sheets in the wind
the night mortars
took out the ammo dump

forever changed
in just a flick of a lighter
scared of our own shadow

five hours later
total devastation controlled
the emotions

helplessness
swept in like a flood

was this real
or a bad dream

tell me
it was a bad dream

vietnamese football

fake pass hand off
75 yards rushing
flag on the play
start over at
20 yard line

cheerleaders in short skirts
bouncy sweaters and pom poms
screaming fans
dense tension
quarterback sends it airborne
end zone td catch
wild crowd
28-21

traded football for m–16
no 75 yards rushing
no flags on the play
no cheerleaders

dense jungle
screaming wounded
dying boys
machine gun chatter
whomp-whomp-whomp
who knows the score

breezes

hot breeze sucks
the breath out of you
first day in-country
don't get it back until
freedom bird takes
you high above the hell
and wings you home

cool breeze plays
on your face
giving life back
to a spent body
time spent in hell
not soon forgotten

warm breeze stirs
the soul to remembrance
of buddies in POW camps
waiting to be rescued
from the hell of torture

still air reminds
the hell warrior
all is not well
with his soul
his country

luring

come to me
my sweet beloved
i will make you forget
        she said

went to her
far from beloved
little less than sweet
        didn't make me forget

she messed with my mind
took what was wrong
        convinced me it was right

rage became a way of life
i wish she could've
        made me forget

raining body parts

stars shine bright
deep into night

sky lights up like
the fourth of july
but it's only march

tracers going
every which way
pretty colors
deadly colors

thoomp, boom, orange
ammo dump's hit

raining fire and dirt
was that a foot
that just hit me

what am i doin' here
please someone
tell me why i'm here

boom

humpin' boonies
stream ahead
caution reigns
shiney goes boom
water runs red
life
washed
downstream

shit

different world

the world
seems like
a million years ago

now

death and destruction
sappers, a-k chatter
punji stakes, claymores
willy pete, hot lz's, mortars

every size kills all

who's in charge

who's in charge here
doesn't anyone know
who's in charge

can't be the arvn
they run away
can't be us
we don't even know
who the damn enemy is

just fire rounds at trees
hoping return fire will
cease and we can go
back to the world

body count reads
like the sunday funnies
six dead-three monkeys
two water buffalo
and one of questionable origin

wasted ammo on animals
how does that read in washington
two hundred dead vc
victory for our side

somebody tell me
who's in charge here

devil two-step

"ebb tide"
used to dance
to that with susie

real close

now i'm dancin'
with the devil
in this hell
called nam

closer than close

sharkey's in
a thousand pieces
half of southern's face
is on sarge's front

nasty s.o.b.'s
uncle sam
uncle ho
do they
give a damn

hell no

mercy

the children
God have mercy
on the children
innocent victims in
man's madness called war

homeless orphans
to grow up with no one
to tell them stories
no one to love them
too young to have
war stories of their own

God have mercy
on the children
with missing arms
or legs, hands or feet
these little ones
paying too great a price
for company in their home

God have mercy
on these children
who will grow up with
fierce hatred or
deep understanding
street smarts
and survival skills
far beyond their innocence

God have mercy on us all

we regret...

river red
washes life
downstream

lifeless eyes
in surprise
stare beyond now

parents visited
'we regret...'

gone yet living
in the special
realm reserved
for warriors

where brothers
embrace him
and regroup

icy fingers

death paints not
a pretty picture
grabs you by the throat
chokes emotions out of you

icy fingers of reality
take over for
a fleeting moment
no time to
deal with loss

screams for mom
amid cries for medic
fear of dying
rides a fast horse

kingdom thine

highway one
ain't no fun

constant sweep
lest we weep

be aware
charlie's snare

claymore mine
kingdom thine

receive us now

death stalks
tiger quick

light in the darkness
not heaven sent
but we are

receive us now
as we come to you
in bits and pieces

splatters of flesh
gray and red

"Our young men, once so handsome and so joyous, taken from us, the son from the mother, the husband from the wife, the dear friend from the dear friend."

Walt Whitman

20 E

DANIEL T KELLEY + WOLFGANG E KRESSE + ROBERT LONGORIA SALINAS + JA
THOMAS E MIDCALF + CHARLES R MILTON JR + ARTHUR C MOURTGIS JR + HO
REINALDO S ORTIZ + GEORGE F PERRY III + DONALD M PETERSON + ROLAND
MARVIN J SINKLER + FRANK TAFOYA + JAMES D WEST + SAMUEL R ALLEN +
GEORGE R ANNOS + ROBERT B BAILEY + ROBERT O BARRY + WILLIAM W BED
LOUIS E BRIZZOLI + GERALD A BROWN + GEORGE R BUTLER + THOMAS W
CLYDE CLARK JR + DELMAR F COOK + STEPHEN J EICHELBERGER + ROSS F FIK
THOMAS J GUARALDI + ARCHIE LEE GUTHRIE + WHILTON A McCARTHY + BENJ
RICHARD H KRUMM + GEORGE R LINDER + DENNIS R HOOKS + RUEBEN J NEAL
GERALD V PARMENTIER + JOHN C PFEIFFER + JAMES L RAY + FREDDIE L ROBI
RALPH D SALERNO + JOHN C SILVER + DWIGHT R STOCKHOLM + DANIEL E TO
HARRY M WADSWORTH + GEORGE H WILLIAMS + RALPH M WIXSON + ROBERT
MICHAEL L BRAEUTIGAN + BENNY LEE BUTLER + EDWARD O CLAEYS + LARR
EUGENE DAWSON + WINFRED ALDERMAN + RONALD W DODGE + CHARLES DO
GEORGE R EDWARDS + LARRY A FAULKNER + JOSEPH O FRIGAULT + WILSON T
STEVEN M HANIOTES + LYNN C HAYES + CLAUDE A HODGE + GARY W HOGLU
CHARLES W JOHNSTON JR + JAMES R MICHAEL + RICHARD L MOORE + JASPER
JOSEPH D PRINCE JR + DON A REDFEARN + ARTHUR REYNOLDS + JOHN E SCHE
TERENCE E SIMON + WENDELL L SLAVENS + GREGORY M THOMPSON + ROGER
WILLIAM C TURNER + JOE L DELONG + CHARLES F ARONHALT JR + JACQUE J
CHRISTOPHER W BEAVERS + WILLIAM A BLACKWELL + ALBERT C BROSE + JA
JOSEPH H CALHOUN + KENNETH R CAMERON + RONALD R CASSEL + KENNETH
EDWARD J CHRISTENSEN + PATRICK J FLAVIN + LOUIS W COLEMAN JR + ESTEB
MARK A DALGLIESH + ALLEN K DEARDEN + CHARLES L ANDERSON + LOUIS D
COIL EDMOND JR + MICHAEL C FARRELL + WILLIAM G FELLINGER JR + WILLIA
JAMES P FITZSIMMONS + STEVE J CHURCHILL + JAMES L FOREMAN + EDWARD
JOHNNIE C FULLER + JOHN C GAINOUS + STANLEY M GODWIN + HORACE R GO
OTTO C GRABOW + BRUCE A GRANDSTAFF + WILLIE R GRIFFITH + CARL R HAL
JOHN W HUDGENS + EDWARD C HULTQUIST + HUGH L HURSTON + COLIN F JAC
CLIFFORD A JOHNSON + RUSSELL F KECK + DANNY E KING + STANLEY S KLEC
DENNIS D KRAMER + RICHARD L LAND + JOE P LARSEN + JOHN W McCOR
ORRIE E MaCOMB JR + CLYDE U MITCHELL + JAMES S LEONARD + BOBBY GENE
THEODORE R NELSON + JEARL E RIMMER + JAMES C OFFLEY + PHILIP J OLOFS
KENNETH D PHARES + CHARLES E RANALLO JR + MICHAEL P RANDALL + CHA
JAMES W ROBBINS + JOHN J ROBERTS + ALFRED W ROBINSON + ROBERT B SAN
MICHAEL SESSA JR + MELVIN L SHIELDS + MARK SMITH JR + MICHAEL F SMIT
CALVIN L TAYLOR + JIMMIE L THOMAS + ROBERT J THOMAS + LELAND H THO
ROBERT A TURNER + OLIVER A WARE + WILLIAM WELLS + JOHN T WILSON + J
PETER ALBERT + KENYON E BEAN + JERRY L BECKHAM + MICHAEL A BODAME
ANTON T BORNSTEIN + ROBERT J BRADY + ROBERT K BRUCE + WILLIE L BROW
WILLIAM J CORBIN + GEDIMINAS J EIDUKAITIS + JAMES W ELDRIGE + DENNI
JAMES F AKINS + REYNALDO S FERNANDEZ + JOHN T FULFORD + WALTER T GE
RAMON GONZALES-RODRIGU + JAMES L GRIFFIN + WAYNE C HARMON + BOBB
HAROLD J HELLBACH + VERNON L HENKE + RICHARD P HILGART + PHILLIP M